gardener's yoga

Bend & Stretch, Dig & Grow

veronica d'orazio
illustrations by tim foss

SASQUATCH BOOKS
SEATTLE

©2006 by Veronica D'Orazio

Printed in Singapore by Star Standard Industries Pte Ltd.
Published by Sasquatch Books
Distributed by Publishers Group West
14 13 12 11 10 09 08 07 06 05   6 5 4 3 2 1

Book design & layout: Kate Basart/Union Pageworks
Illustrations: Tim Foss

ISBN 1-57061-466-0

Library of Congress Cataloging-in-Publication Data is available.

Sasquatch Books | 119 South Main Street, Suite 400 | Seattle, WA 98104 | 206/467-4300
www.sasquatchbooks.com | custserv@sasquatchbooks.com

contents

introduction

❋ **when i used to weed the garden,** I would enter some kind of bizarre green vortex where time seemed to stop. I experienced a strange, almost physical compulsion to clear and continue. I loved the satisfying, sensual thrill of pulling stubborn weeds, their root structures still perfectly intact, neatly from the damp rich soil and hurling them toward the compost heap. I used to take it too far, however. I would weed unceasingly. I forgot to eat. I forgot to socialize. Mostly, I forgot my body. I would squat for three hours straight under the squash blossoms and then try to stand up. Stooped over and sore, I would hobble over to the hose and start watering. Quasimodo of the daffodils. Hunchback of the hostas.

And it didn't stop with the weeding. Taxing my body was so seemingly part of gardening work that for years it didn't really occur to me to address the aches and pains. Like most gardeners, the physical demands were (and often still are) superseded by the persistent, unwavering need to grow things. Gardeners will ignore alarms of pain and fatigue to reach, lean, bend, lift, haul, and carry our visions of the dream garden to fruition.

❋ **april 1997 was the clincher.** It was spring and I was buzzing with plans. Operation Pollination. I spent days at a time plotting, scheming, and preparing my perfect picture of a prelapsarian paradise: a lush, wild Eden dripping with verdant greens, cool whites, shocking pinks. Sunbursts of red and gold, hushed hues of lavender and cerulean.

5

I did nothing else for days. Hours passed, the sun crossed the sky, lowered, and set, and when I finally stopped working, it was not because I wanted to: It was because I couldn't stand up. My back went out somewhere in the scented geraniums and no redolent lure of "attar of roses" was going to bring me to my knees again. I hobbled inside and found my heating pad.

I had been studying yoga for a few years by that time and, lying on my back breathing through the soreness caused by spring weeding, I started plotting my return to the garden plot. I began exploring the ways in which yoga could support the gardener's craft, whereas before my yoga practice had been distinct from my gardening work. Instead of yoga acting mostly as a form of physical damage control after the aches and pains of gardening had set in, I began to see how clearly yoga could prevent further injury, bolster my strength and flexibility in the garden, and act as a gentle reminder to breathe mindfulness into the physical work a garden demands.

❋ as both my love of yoga and my love of gardening have continued over the years, the links between these two pursuits continue to unfold. The practice of yoga and the practice of gardening are more closely connected to each other than one may realize. Even the language of yoga echoes the gardener's craft. Yogis talk of rooting through the feet, of grounding through the sitting bones, of blooming the heart center skyward. Many of the Sanskrit names for the postures, dating back more than two thousand years, originate from a deep reverence and respect for the natural world: Tree Pose. Mountain. Blooming Lotus. Many of the poses are named after animals, reminding us of not only our connection to other creatures, but also of our similarities to them: Lion Pose. Rabbit. Cobra. The posture *Ustrasana*, or Camel, for example, is not simply a backbend;

it also links us metaphorically to the energy reserves stored within our own bodies, just as the camel can go for miles and miles without water. The most well-known *vinyasa* (a flowing series of postures guided by the breath) is the *Surya Namaskar*, or Sun Salutation, a rhythmic sequencing that constitutes a kind of moving prayer, an homage to photosynthesis, a way of giving thanks to the life-giving power of the sun. A profound love for and celebration of life and death is at the core of yogic philosophy, and this same love and celebration is, of course, the force behind all gardeners everywhere.

Gardening is a kind of moving meditation, a direct and physical communion with the seasons, with the sun and the moon and the elements. To garden is to participate in, nurture, and witness the cycles of life and death on this planet and to witness closely nature's astonishing beauty and growth. Of course, lest I wax too romantic, gardening is also at times pure drudgery. Hours and hours pass grooming and preparing the beds, and at the end of the day often we see only the slightest evidence of our efforts. We stake two rows of fragile, delicate sweet peas and then a sudden rain comes and hammers them to the ground. Exasperating. The number of damp, sticky dead blooms that cling to the petunias, the geraniums, the begonias! Deadheading alone can be a Sisyphean strain on even the most patient gardener.

Fortunately the dilemmas and demands of the garden are always beautifully upstaged by the daily miracles of growth and change. We go to the garden willingly, joyfully. As such, the garden becomes not only a source of life and nourishment and beauty, but also a sacred space that centers, uplifts, and grounds the gardener in one's life and in one's self.

Yoga, like gardening, is at its roots a profoundly fundamental practice: The gardener plants a seed and watches it grow. As the seed grows, the gardener tends, nourishes, protects, and welcomes the results of his or her efforts. For a student of yoga, the process is the same: The seed of yoga is the breath. We plant the seed—our attention to and witnessing of the breath—and nourish the body, mind, and soul from this base.

how to use this book

✳ *gardener's yoga* contains a series of postures tailored for soothing the typical aches and pains associated with gardening. The aim of this book is to foster awareness of breath, posture, and careful movement as the gardener works. The postures I have chosen can also serve as a general introduction to the study of yoga for those who have never practiced it before. I have included twenty-one poses using a *vinyasa* style, or flow, with each pose smoothly transitioning into the next. The book is divided into three sections, each containing seven postures, ideally divided into the three series that you do before, during, and after gardening.

I encourage you to choose from one or all of the poses on any given day. Pick and choose from different sections, choosing your own flow, or practicing a posture here and there as needed while you move through your gardening work. Within each pose description, I have listed the main areas of the body that benefit, but remember yoga is a holistic approach to exercise: Even though Legs-up-the-Wall Pose is listed as stretching the back and legs, for example, it is also is a curative for headaches, insomnia, fatigue, varicose veins, and more.

Yoga should be the one form of exercise that is not intimidating. The great yogi T. K. V. Desikachar has said that anyone who can breathe can do yoga: that means all of us. I invite you to practice the series here in its entirety and then, when you feel comfortable with the poses, experiment with the sequencing on your own. As a general rule, a strong yoga practice encourages the spine to move in all directions, incorporating forward bends and backbends, lateral stretches and twists.

You should also have a blend of simple, easy postures as well as some that gently challenge and encourage you to go further in your abilities. If a pose is difficult for you (but not painful or harming the body in any way), this may be a cue not to resist but to explore further. Many gardeners have tight hips, for instance, from the hours spent planting and weeding. Thus, when you first encounter a hip opener, you may be surprised by the struggle and avoid the pose completely after that. Instead, however, consider resistance or blockages as your body's request for help or attention. After all, when a young or fragile plant is struggling, you support it by staking or coiling wire around the base. You should also give the same nurturance and gentle support to yourself. Tending the garden and tending the body is the same practice.

breaking ground

sometimes getting started is the hardest part of gardening. The ground may be cold and hard; it may or may not have adequate drainage or good soil. It seems impossible to know where to start; what needs to be done seems endless. Start from your own center. Breathe and gently open the body and focus the mind for the day's demands. This will help your garden grow more than even the highest-grade mulch! The seven poses listed in this section can be done before you begin gardening. These poses will gently warm up the spine and prepare the back, hips, legs, and knees for the day's work.

easy seat pose

(Sukhasana)

breath, knees, and hips
Regardless of how light or heavy your gardening work may be on any given day, take time to sit quietly before you begin. In this simple, crossed-legged position, awareness is drawn to the whole body. Easy Seat allows you to acknowledge and identify any tension or discomfort in the body. Focus on your breath. Observe your thoughts and direct your attention toward the present. This meditative seat will greatly increase your concentration, vigor, and creativity as you garden.

1. Sit comfortably in a cross-legged position, with your sitting bones evenly distributed on the ground.
2. Sit up straight, with your shoulders gliding away from the ears and the collarbones widening. Relax your knees, hips, and feet.
3. Rest your hands on the knees, and focus on your breath. Allow your breath to lengthen naturally, moving through the front and back of the body.
4. Allow thoughts to come and go. Inhale and exhale slowly. Return your mind again and again to the sound and feeling of the breath whenever distractions arise.

tip For greater ease and comfort in Easy Seat Pose, sit on the edge of a pillow or bolster, allowing the pelvis to tip forward slightly and the spine to lengthen. Place pillows under the knees for added support.

cobbler's pose

(Baddha Konasana)

hips, back, and knees Cobbler's Pose gently opens the hips and stretches the back. It subtly opens the heart, relaxes the knees, and is a nice preparation for, and counter pose to, hours spent kneeling and squatting in the garden.

1. From Easy Seat Pose, bring the soles of the feet together. Pull your feet close to your body. Grip the big toes with your thumbs and index fingers.
2. Pull up on your toes and extend your chest out over the feet, keeping the spine long. Resist rounding the shoulders. Instead, keep the chest open, the collarbones wide, and breathe into the back of the heart.
3. Use your elbows to gently press the inner thighs away from one another and send the knees closer to the earth.

tip If you are highly flexible or are recovering from a groin injury, stay in Cobbler's Pose, but draw your knees toward one another as you resist them isometrically with your elbows. This will strengthen the hip region.

cat-cow pose

(*Chakravakasana*)

back and shoulders

The Cat-Cow Pose will warm up your spine and get you ready for all the reaching, bending, and lifting that is part of gardening work. Arching and rounding the back releases and strengthens the spine, back, shoulders, and belly. It is an ideal warm-up exercise, and it will also provide immediate relief when you find yourself sitting, kneeling, or standing in one position for too long.

1. From Cobbler's Pose, transition to all fours. Place your hands under your shoulders and your knees at hip distance. Gently draw your navel toward the spine and lengthen the body from the crown of the head to the tailbone.

2. **Cow:** On inhalation, arch the spine, drop your belly toward the earth, and extend the heart and tailbone skyward. Track your shoulders away from the ears and look up, forehead smooth. Keep your face and neck relaxed and inhale through the entire body.

3. **Cat:** On exhalation, round the back and strongly draw your navel toward the spine. Press firmly through your hands and feet. Drop your head and gaze toward your navel.

4. Move smoothly from Cow to Cat at your own pace, inhaling to lift up, exhaling to round.

tip For sensitive knees, place a blanket underneath them for extra padding.

child's pose

(Balasana)

back and hips Nurturing and grounding, Child's Pose soothes the whole body. The back and spine are gently stretched. The shoulders release and soften toward the floor. The neck, belly, and hips relax. The knees soften, the backs of the feet are gently stretched, and the heart rate naturally slows in this pose, calming your entire being. What better way to prepare for rototilling?

1. From the Cat-Cow Pose, shift your weight back onto the heels and drape the upper body over the thighs. Rest your forehead on the ground and place your hands beside your ankles.
2. Relax your shoulders over the thighs; relax your hips toward the heels.
3. Inhale deeply to stretch the long muscles of the back. Exhale deeply to release through the shoulders, pelvis, and feet.

tip If this pose is difficult, widen the knees, beyond hip distance. Place your hands beside your legs, and rest your head to the right and the left for equal duration.

downward-facing dog

(*Adho Mukha Shvanasana*)

back, shoulders, and legs
Hauling fifty-pound bags of manure up a garden path is no picnic. Gardeners are like bamboo: We need to be both strong and pliant to prosper. The overall effect of this pose is to strengthen and stretch the legs, belly, back, and shoulders. It will bolster your efforts as you begin your work, and it is an excellent way to release the head and neck after hours spent deadheading or planting with your head in front of your shoulders.

1. From Child's Pose, reach the arms forward and place your hands parallel to one another at shoulder distance. Transition onto all fours.
2. From all fours, shift the pelvis up and back. With head down and palms flat, reach the chest toward the ground, lift the sitting bones, and move the heels back and down.

tip For sensitive wrists, bring the forearms to the ground instead, parallel with the shoulders, and lengthen the legs away from the forearms, with the heels lowering.

standing forward bend

(Uttanasana)

legs, chest, shoulders, and low back
Staking may get the clematis climbing, but it also plants the seeds for stiffness, especially in the upper body. This pose, with the added benefit of being a chest opener, will relax the head, neck, and shoulders. Lacing the hands behind the back will further open the upper body. Tight hamstrings cause a great deal of the back pain gardeners experience. Standing Forward Bends lengthen and stretch the hamstrings and will, in turn, release tension in the back and sacrum.

1. From Downward-Facing Dog, walk the feet to the hands. Let the big toe mounds and the ankles touch.
2. Bend forward, interlace fingers behind back. Evenly distribute weight in the center of both feet.
3. Relax the weight of your head, neck, and shoulders. Lift your arms toward the sky, gaze up toward the navel, and deepen your breathing.

tip   For tight hamstrings, bend your knees generously and hold opposite elbows.

mountain pose

(*Tadasana*)

balance, feet, shoulders, and back

Mindful standing is one of the most relaxing and nourishing exercises a gardener can practice. Mountain Pose is deceptively simple. Sometimes referred to as "active" or "engaged" standing, it encourages good posture and gives us a chance to notice poor postural habits such as rounded shoulders or hyperextension of the lower back or leaning weight on one hip while we water the garden. A strong Mountain Pose reminds us of our connection to the earth as we root strongly through our feet, symbolically and energetically receiving sustenance and strength from the ground beneath us. We send this sustenance and strength to all parts of the body, as we stand with awareness.

1. From Standing Forward Bend, slowly unroll the spine vertebra by vertebra until standing tall, feet slightly parted.
2. Relax your arms at your side and glide the shoulder blades down the back.
3. Eyes closed, cultivate a deliberate, conscious experience of standing. As in a seated meditation, this pose has a quiet devotional aspect to it and will subtly energize and restore your entire being.

tip For a more active Mountain Pose and to strengthen the calves and feet, turn your palms out, rotating your thumbs away from your body. Rise up onto your heels, balancing. Lower and repeat several times.

planting seeds

halfway through your gardening work, take time out to check in with your body and see how you are feeling. When we are most absorbed in our gardening tasks, we are most likely to ignore signs of physical discomfort. Make it a habit to stop your work, breathe, attend to your body's needs, and you will resume gardening with increased energy, ease, and focus. The seven postures listed in this section emphasize breathing, balance, and release. They will support you as you continue with your tasks, and give you time to undo some of the tension and soreness that you have built up.

upward-reaching hands

(*Urdhva Hastasana*)

back and shoulders

How often do you stop in the midst of gardening to stretch and breathe? Reaching the arms overhead connects you immediately to the power of inhalation and exhalation. Moving through a rhythmic, steady flow is very balancing to all the body's systems. This energizes and renews us as we move through our tasks with beauty and grace, reestablishing breath awareness and inner peace.

1. From Mountain Pose, reach the arms out to the side and then overhead. Place your palms together and look up toward the sky.

2. Plant evenly through both feet and work toward straightening the elbows.

3. On exhalation, draw the palms together in prayer position and bring them to the heart center.

4. Repeat this flow four to six times at your own pace, inhaling the arms above the head, exhaling them back to prayer position.

tip If your shoulders feel hunched or sore in this pose, widen the arms to shoulder distance and practice the extension from there.

tree pose

(*Vrikshasana*)

balance, legs, and postural strengthening
Although trees are anchored by their roots, supported by their strong, thick trunks, they are in constant motion. Subtle changes in the wind cause them to sway or bow. Heavy storms rattle their boughs, and yet they maintain their centers. Balancing postures are dynamic and fluid, with continuous subtle movements felt in the spine and limbs. Think of your feet as roots reaching deep down into the soil, sending out support and stability in all directions, drinking up vital energy from the earth and transferring it to the whole body.

1. From Upward-Reaching Hands, transfer weight into your right side. Engage your low belly muscles, lift the right foot off the floor, and place it on the left upper inner thigh.

2. Place your hands in prayer position at the heart and press your foot toward the thigh and your thigh toward the foot. When steady, extend the prayer hands overhead, elbows straight.

3. Do not grip the floor with the toes of your supporting foot. Rather, root through the sole of the foot and engage the calf muscle for added balance.

4. Hold for several breath cycles and repeat on the opposite side.

tip If you feel wobbly, bring your arms out to the side instead. You can also practice this balance by keeping your toes on the floor and placing the raised foot just inside the ankle area.

standing heart opener

(Urdhva Mukhasana)

legs, chest, and shoulders
We can cultivate mindfulness and tranquility in still poses and take these gifts into our active gardening endeavors. Instead of slouching or leaning your weight on one hip when you water, for example, let the standing poses in this section remind you to stand strong and upright. In the variation described here, attention is also drawn to the heart center, opening the front of the chest, allowing the shoulders to open as well.

1. From Tree Pose, stand with your feet at hip distance. Bring your hands behind your back. Interlace fingers behind back and squeeze the shoulders blades toward one another. Draw your woven hands toward the tailbone. Widen through the collarbones and deepen the breath.

2. Keep your head in line with your shoulders and reach the elbows away from one another. Breathe deeply into the front of the chest.

tip Keep a subtle bend in your elbows to protect the joints and focus the opening on the chest and shoulders.

moon pose

(Chandrasana)

back and shoulders

Vines are the best teachers when it comes to lateral movement. Consider how passion vine travels sideways through space for several inches, intrepid, and steadfast, before stopping to coil around a fence or trellis. Lateral stretches bring flexibility and suppleness to the spine and counteract a gardener's tendency to keep the spine in a fixed position for too long. These stretches have an energizing effect on the body and naturally inspire the breath to deepen.

1. From Standing Heart Opener, place the left hand on your hip. Straighten the right arm toward sky.
2. Lean to the left, reaching your right arm in line with your ear. Engage your low belly to support the low back as you side bend.
3. Stay long through the left waist, using your hand on your hip to support the stretch.
4. Repeat on the opposite side.

tip To deepen the pose, bring both arms overhead, parallel with one another as you side bend.

garland pose

hips and low back

Because the gardener is of course no stranger to the squat, this variation is done with the legs wide, to foster mobility in the hips, while at the same time lengthening the spine. The gentle traction of the elbows at the inner thighs releases tension in the groin and allows the shoulder blades to relax and glide down the back. Unlike the squatting we engage in while gardening, this pose counters the tendency gardeners have to round their shoulders and lower their heads—thus putting strain on the neck muscles—while working.

1. From Moon Pose, bring your feet wider than hip distance. Come into a squat with the knees wide.

2. Bring your hands to a prayer pose, using the elbows to gently open the knees.

3. Instead of rounding, lengthen through the spine and lift through the crown of the head, relaxing your shoulders and hips. Continue applying gentle pressure on the knees to deepen the squat.

tip If your heels don't touch the floor, roll up the back of your mat or place a blanket under your feet to balance.

seated spinal twist

(Marichysana)

low back Think of how ivy wraps around the trunk of a tree: This is a good image for seated twists. Our trunks, or spines, should stay as straight as possible while we rotate or twist like the ivy around this strong central axis. Twists cleanse the internal organs. They stimulate digestion, increase circulation, bolster the immune system, and help move toxins and stress out of the body. They are powerful, clearing postures that promote good health. This seated twist helps to mobilize the spine and release tension in the low back and neck.

1. From Garland Pose, find your way to sitting. Straighten your right leg, allowing the foot to flex strongly, toes in a straight line. Bring your left knee to your body, resting your foot on the ground.

2. Hug your right arm around your left knee and twist to your left. Sitting up tall, gaze to the far left corner of your vision.

3. Repeat on the opposite side.

tip To deepen the pose, bring your right elbow outside of your left knee instead; repeat on the opposite side.

bridge pose

(Setu Bandha Sarvangasana)

back, hips, and legs
Gardeners spend a lot of time bending over: Bridge Pose to the rescue! It is a gentle backbend, and backbends are by nature very energizing. This pose stretches the back and the neck, opens the hips, and strengthens the quadriceps. Lie on a flat, even section of the yard when you practice the pose outside. Bridge will restore suppleness in your spine and will help relieve low back and hip tension.

1. From Seated Spinal Twist, lie down on your back. Bend your knees and place your feet on the floor at hip distance or slightly wider. Place your hands beside your hips.

2. On inhalation, press down through the feet and slowly lift the hips toward the sky, unrolling the spine one vertebra at a time.

3. Gently press the back of the head against the ground, allowing for space between the chin and the chest.

4. Slowly roll down on exhalation. Repeat and hold or move through a flow as you wish.

tip Resist letting the low back do all the work here. Strongly engage your feet and thighs to lift the hips. Use your belly, drawing the navel toward the spine (not only will this strengthen your core muscles, it will also allow you to lengthen through the tailbone).

harvest time

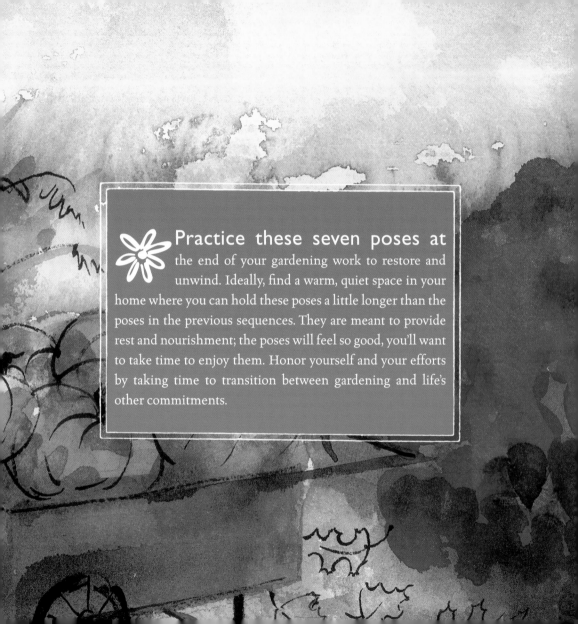

Practice these seven poses at the end of your gardening work to restore and unwind. Ideally, find a warm, quiet space in your home where you can hold these poses a little longer than the poses in the previous sequences. They are meant to provide rest and nourishment; the poses will feel so good, you'll want to take time to enjoy them. Honor yourself and your efforts by taking time to transition between gardening and life's other commitments.

knees-to-chest pose

(*Apanasana*)

sacrum and knees Just as many flowers slowly close in on themselves when the light fades, this posture brings us back to our center, fostering introspection and reminding us to slow down, breathe, and quiet the mind. Here the entire back, hips, and legs are soothed and rejuvenated. It is an excellent pose to find throughout the gardener's day when the body feels tight or tired, and it restores the body after physical work of any kind. It is one of the easiest ways to get in touch with your breath, as the action of drawing the knees toward the chest inspires an often spontaneous deep, slow exhalation.

1. From Bridge Pose, bring your knees in toward the chest and interlace your fingers around the fronts of the knees.
2. Relax the back of the neck, spine, and sacrum. Soften through the tops of the shoulders and release any effort in the lower legs and feet.

tip If lacing your fingers around the fronts of the knees is difficult, place your hands underneath the knees instead or rest your hands on top of the knees, creating more space between your belly and your thighs.

supine twist

(Jathara Parivatanasana)

middle and lower back Like clearing a patch of weeds from a bed, this pose is a healthy take on instant gratification! Similar to the Seated Spinal Twist, the rejuvenating power of this pose is limitless. This is one of the easiest poses to be completely passive in and is even milder than the seated version. Once the knees bend and drop to each side, serenity is all that is needed.

1. From Knees-to-Chest Pose, inhale and widen your arms away from one another, palms up.

2. On exhalation, keep both shoulders on the ground and lower your knees to your right side.

3. Turn your head in the opposite direction of the knees, looking out over the left fingertips as you deepen the breath.

4. Repeat on the opposite side.

tip If your knees do not reach the floor in this twist, place a pillow or folded blanket under them for support.

happy baby pose

(Ananda Balasana)

low back, hips, and knees
Happy Baby Pose not only soothes the back and opens the hips, it also allows the feet and knees to revitalize. Widening the knees out to the side of the torso is a much needed counter pose to the hours spent putting weight on our knees to weed and plant. This is a joyful pose—the name alone should make you smile.

1. From Supine Twist, bring your knees toward your chest. Lift your feet into the air and hold onto the bottoms of your feet with your hands.

2. Relax the head, neck, and shoulders along the ground. Bring your feet parallel with the knees and widen the knees away from one another.

3. Use your hands to press your knees strongly toward the earth, with your feet strongly flexed toward the sky.

tip Place a blanket underneath your hips for extra padding.

goddess pose
(Supta Baddha Konasana)

hips, shoulders, and neck
The shape of this pose reminds me of day lilies, their petals so triumphantly open, star-shaped and lovely. Goddess Pose gently opens the hips and relaxes the legs and back. Bringing the arms overhead will foster deeper breathing and help the upper body to relax as well. Be lily-like in your practicing of this pose: Give yourself plenty of time to unfold.

1. From Happy Baby Pose, bring the soles of the feet together and press the knees toward the ground.
2. Inhale and bring the arms overhead, resting the backs of your hands on the ground. Join your thumb and index fingers together and press your elbows away from one another.
3. Relax the back of the body along the ground and soften your belly.

tip For a variation on this pose, incorporate a mild backbend by placing a bolster behind your sitting bones. Lie down on your back, resting your weight on the bolster as the arms come overhead. Blankets or pillows can be placed under your knees for extra support.

thread-the-needle pose

hips, knees, and sacrum
If you're like many gardeners, your hips may feel especially compromised by the end of your day's work. You will feel a strong release and deep stretch through the backs of the hips and the buttocks from this pose. This is a powerful posture; don't be surprised if it feels more intense than the other ones listed in this series. Approach the pose in a slow, steady manner and let your body open to it by degrees.

1. From Goddess Pose, cross your right foot over your left knee. Weave your arms through your legs, interlacing your fingers around the front of the left knee.
2. Relax the head, neck, and shoulders on the floor. Gently pull the knee toward your body, keeping the low back and sacrum on the floor.
3. Repeat on the opposite side.

tip If your hands don't reach around the knee, hold onto the outside of the raised foot instead.

legs-up-the-wall pose

(*Viparita Karani*)

legs and back   Practice this pose often and you will have more energy for even the most daunting of gardening projects. This partial inversion reverses the effects of gravity, slows down the aging process, boosts the immune system and increases circulation in the legs, all while gently stretching the back.

1. From Thread-the-Needle Pose, roll to your side and bring your mat and/or blanket to a wall.
2. Sit with your legs facing the wall. Carefully roll on to your back, and walk your legs up the wall, making sure the hips are in line with the baseboard.
3. Rest the whole length of the spine along the floor. Rest your arms at your side or over your head, palms facing up. Allow the chin to lift gently away from the chest to support the natural curve of the neck.

tip   If your low back is uncomfortable in this pose, bring your hips farther away from the wall so there is space between your body and the baseboard. You can also use any additional props to soften the pose, such as a bolster underneath the hips or a blanket roll for underneath the neck.

note   Because this pose reverses the flow of blood in the body, do not practice it during menstruation or if you have high blood pressure or glaucoma.

corpse pose/final relaxation

(*Shvanasana*)

body and mind
We participate in the cycles of life and death in the garden. Corpse Pose is both a death and rebirth: Done at the end of any posture series, Corpse allows the body and mind to absorb the benefits of your practice. When we emerge from the pose, we feel as transformed and revitalized as the cherry blossoms opening again after winter's end.

1. From Legs-up-the-Wall, roll to your side to come out of the pose. Lie flat on your back and bring your legs slightly wider than hip distance.

2. Bring your arms to your side and extend them about six to eight inches away from your body, allowing the shoulders to open and relax.

3. Make sure that you are even through the left and right sides of your body and relax your weight toward the earth.

4. Close your eyes and breathe deeply. When distractions arise, concentrate on the breath. Begin at the crown of the head and relax every part of the body, all the way down to the tips of the toes. Be perfectly still.

tip
For extra back support, place a bolster or folded blanket under your knees. You can also make a narrow blanket roll for under your neck.

sowing the seeds
of contentment

on ambiance and aromatherapy

like gardening, yoga is a solitary practice. It is a practice of self-study, or *svadhyaya*. Find a place in your home free of distractions. Take time to be alone without the phone, stereo, computer, or housemates interfering. A clutter-free space in your house will further ground you for your practice. Light candles to soften the room's ambiance and foster a tranquil heart. Most important, bring the garden into your practice.

1. **Cut herbs such as lavender, rosemary,** or scented geranium and place them in a small vase or bowl nearby while you practice. You can also take a handful of your favorite aromatic herb and rub your palms together vigorously, inhaling the lovely scent at the start of your seated meditation. Use lavender to calm or uplift, rosemary to energize, or rose geranium to steady your nerves. Make or purchase an eye pillow filled with lavender or any other aromatic herb that you choose and place it over your eyes in final relaxation. Herbal eye pillows not only soothe the eyes, they also release tension in the face and body, quiet the mind, and lift your spirits if you are feeling susceptible to emotional unease.

2. **Fresh flowers from the garden** are a wonderful addition to your yoga practice. Place them on a small table or, if you wish, make an altar that you can see while you are moving through your postures. Flowers are often used as tools for meditation, focusing the mind on the beauty in the here and now. Try floating a blossom in a bowl and use this lovely sight as a centering tool in your meditation. My first meditation teacher says he learned to meditate by staring at a single flower. The beauty and the complexity of a flower keeps the mind centered and alert. With practice, the boundaries between yourself and the flower begin to break down. Flowers show us how to just be.

3. Use essential oils or flower essences to enhance your practice. Sprinkle a few drops of essential oil, such as ylang-ylang or rose geranium, in votive holders, allowing the candles' heat to bring out subtle fragrances while you practice. After the end of a practice, take a hot bath and float blossoms in the water to enhance the beauty of unwinding. Try using one or a few of your favorite oils in the bath for further relaxation. Mix a pint of half-and-half or heavy cream with ten to fifteen drops of one or more essential oils. The cream and oils will emulsify and, when added to your bath water, help your body to more fully absorb the fragrance and healing benefits of the oils.

gardener's yoga positions

Back	Cobbler's	Cat-Cow	Child's	Downward-Facing Dog	Standing Forward Bend	Mountain	Upward-Reaching Hands	Moon
Knees	Easy Seat		Cobbler's	Mountain	Garland	Knees-to-Chest		
Hips	Easy Seat	Cobbler's	Child's		Garland	Bridge	Happy Baby	
Legs		Downward-Facing Dog	Standing Forward Bend		Mountain	Tree	Standing Heart Opener	
Shoulders	Cat-Cow	Downward-Facing Dog	Standing Forward Bend	Mountain		Upward-Reaching Hands	Standing Heart Opener	Moon
Neck	Standing Forward Bend		Mountain	Goddess		Corpse		
Chest	Standing Forward Bend		Standing Heart Opener		Garland	Corpse		

Garland	Seated Spinal Twist	Bridge	Knees-to-Chest	Supine Twist	Happy Baby	Thread-the-Needle	Legs-up-the-Wall	Corpse
Happy Baby			Thread-the-Needle			Corpse		
		Goddess	Thread-the-Needle					
Bridge	Legs-up-the-Wall			Corpse				
		Seated Spinal Twist	Goddess	Corpse				

63

about the author

✳ **veronica d'orazio** is a certified yoga instructor, writer, and floral designer. She has spent the last ten years striving for balance between these three interests. Tree pose helps. She most recently wrote the text for *Fleurish*, published by Sasquatch Books. She lives in Seattle, Washington, where she also moonlights as a gardener in her friends' backyards.

about the illustrator

✳ **tim foss** is an illustrator and ceramic artist currently living in Seattle. He won the 2004 Poncho Recognition Award through the Seattle Art Museum for his outstanding illustrated work in ceramics. He first discovered yoga about ten years ago and has been practicing ever since, but he's been weeding gardens and eating fresh zucchini bread ever since he could walk. For more images of his work, visit www.timothyfoss.com.